I0511006

Published by A.Michelle Blakeley
www.simplicitymastered.com

Cover image: Alexander Kharchenko

For information contact
PO Box 5944
Sacramento, California 95817
www.simplicitymastered.com

Book design by A.Michelle Blakeley

ISBN-10: 1633185850
ISBN-13: 9781633185852

First Edition: March 2015

10 9 8 7 6 5 4 3 2 1

Acknowledgements

They say behind every great man, is a strong woman. Well, behind this strong woman, is a great man. My husband Brady has been incredibly supportive throughout my entrepreneurial journey. He's even been crazy enough to partner with me on a few ventures. Marriage and business can work together. I'm grateful for his insight and honored with his love.

For every client who was brave enough to take that first step and strong enough to continue the journey, my trials and errors are for your benefit.

Table of Contents

ZERO

60

Introduction

I'm a professional boot-strapper and serial entrepreneur. I've sold real estate, owned a nightclub, a transitional living facility, founded a solar cleaning start-up, established a micro business therapy practice and 4 years ago I opened a contemporary art gallery in less than 90 days. I'm currently working on a new project for women entrepreneurs.

I've made a lot of mistakes and I've had a lot of successes. I say all of that because, from experience, I know what it takes to get a business off the ground, efficiently, effectively and with minimal resources. I know how to start, run and grow small businesses. So much so, that I can show YOU how to start a business, implement a productive system and get traction in 60 days or less.

Starting a business is not about everything being perfect with all the stars and moon being aligned. It's about taking advantage of an opportunity to provide something that people are willing to pay for. No more, no less. If people don't want to buy what you're selling, there's no business. So, a lot of what you read about starting a business is irrelevant until you cover that. Once you know you have something that people are willing to pay for, cover the fundamentals to get yourself into the market. It's the fundamentals that allow you to open up shop and you make continuous adjustments from there.

Mind you, having the fundamentals doesn't guarantee you success, but it does put you in a better position to achieve success. There are so many resources available on how to start a business, yet, people still overlook the fundamentals and businesses continue to fail at an alarming rate. Things are very fluid in a new business. You need to be able to make changes as you learn what is working and what is not working.

The market and people are fickle. What's *in* today could be in tomorrow's trash. So, understand that you have no control. Entrepreneurship is not for the faint at heart or people who think it would be "fun." Owning a business is not just about putting "CEO" on your business cards and making your own hours. The ebb and flow of getting a business started, sustained and scaled has wreaked havoc on the strongest of marriages, the best of friendships and the soundest of minds.

I don't mean to scare you away from starting a business, but I do want you to be mentally prepared for what could easily be waiting for you around the corner. Think carefully about what you are about to undertake.

1 Concept

Ideas won't keep. Something must be done about them.

- Alfred North Whitehead

Concept

Great ideas aren't so great when someone else has already beat you to the punch… the market doesn't exist … or it's too small to scale.

We all have ideas. Entrepreneurs act on them. They take action to make them happen, sometimes at extreme odds. They mitigate their fears and risks with due diligence and faith. The only thing that separates you from starting a business and entrepreneurs who already have is …action. You will never know what will or won't work or be successful until you take that first step. Everything after that is trial and error because even calculated risks can yield devastating results.

Viability, feasibility and due diligence

Do your homework. Google the mess out of your idea. Search the Internet high and low for your idea, fragments of your idea and keywords. Keep in mind, just because your idea is taken, doesn't mean you should give up. Sometimes ideas can be altered, sometimes they can be improved on and sometimes they can be turned on their head.

(See appendix for "Why You Can't Be Like Steve Jobs, Richard Branson or Mark Cuban")

Do you have the time, energy and resources needed to give your business the attention it needs? There is a lot of work to be done. You could work your new business as a side hustle, but be mindful of timing. Are you at risk of someone beating you to market? How much time can you realistically devote to the business? Do you need a partner or assistant to help you get started? How will you address your knowledge and skills gaps?

Fleshing out your business concept is what stands between your idea and your business plan - working out the possibilities in detail. Here are some things to consider when you are working through a business concept:

Vision – What does the execution of your purpose look like?

Mission – Why are you in business?

Values – What will your business stand for?

Brand Identity – How will your business look?

Objective – What purpose does your business serve?

Strategy – How will you accomplish your objective?

Industry – What position will you play in the market? Where is the industry headed?

Product – Should you license your product/idea or keep it in-house?

Manufacturing - Can it be manufactured/produced at a reasonable price point?

Service – Are your costs competitive?

Client – Whom will you serve?

You – What skillset and knowledge to you possess?

Money – What are the costs and can you generate revenue?

Exit – What is the end game for you and your business?

How you respond to these questions will help you determine *if* you should proceed and how you should proceed. Niche businesses and businesses with clearly identified and strong competitive advantages are the ones that survive and thrive. If your business doesn't do something truly different to set itself apart from competitors or the market you are trying to serve is too small to scale, you'll want to reconsider your business idea. In addition, if the costs are insurmountable or your intellectual property is at risk of duplication or invalidation, you'll want to reconsider your options.

Define success

Determine what success will look like for you from the start because it's not always about money. Sometimes it's about flexibility. It's about social contributions. It could be political. It could be environmental stewardship. Success looks different to different people.

Purpose and passion

What is your purpose?

How does your concept relate to your purpose and passion? Does your business idea support your innate purpose and passion? Businesses that support the owner's purpose provide an extra level of focus and strength. Your purpose is something that you feel you were born to do and provide. It doesn't change. It's part of who you are. Passion can change. It's like lust. You're all over it one day and the next, not so much.

It's great to be passionate about what you're doing, but people don't pay for passion. They pay for what they need, what they want, value, time-savers, money-savers, etc.

Put the **EXTRA** in your concept by building a list of anticipated buyers and testing your market first. Set up a landing page; drive traffic to the page (via social media posts and paid ad, Facebook ads, Twitter ads or Google ads). You can also start a crowdfunding/marketing campaign and take pre-sales. Be sure to keep your subscribers updated on the progress of your product and launch.

Concept Checklist

- ☐ Does this idea already exist? If so, what is your demonstrable value improvement?
- ☐ If no, can you patent, trademark or copyright your idea?
- ☐ Is there sufficient and proven demand for your product or service?
- ☐ What problem are you solving? What is the consumer pain?
- ☐ Why is this problem worth solving?
- ☐ What alternatives are people using to meet their needs or are they going without?
- ☐ Who are your competitors?
- ☐ Who will buy your product or service?
- ☐ Why will they buy your product or service?
- ☐ Who is your ideal customer?
- ☐ What can you do to capture realistic market share?
- ☐ What is the "all-in" cost to produce your product?
- ☐ What is your business model?
- ☐ Will this business support the lifestyle you want?
- ☐ What asset or capability are you bringing that is unique?
- ☐ If your product is new, how will you validate the need for your product?
- ☐ How can you test and learn before building a full business?
- ☐ Can you test your product and get client feedback?
- ☐ Can you deliver on client expectations?
- ☐ Can you market your business through existing channels?
- ☐ Can you leverage online marketing and social media to scale the business?
- ☐ What is your revenue model?

☐ What key activities generate revenue?
☐ Will your business produce gross margins of at least 50% and/or net margins of at least 20%
☐ What resources do you have access to?
☐ Does your business require an investor or business loan?
☐ What does the future of your market look like? How will competition change?
☐ What is your exit strategy?
☐ Can this business be sold as an exit strategy?
☐ How does your business relate to your purpose?
☐ Are you passionate about the business?
☐ Will you still be running the business 5 years from now?
☐ Will others be passionate or excited about your business?
☐ Is your business appropriate for an incubator or accelerator?
☐ Could you benefit from a business partner?
☐ Do you have a mentor?
☐ Do you have an accountability partner?

2 Advisory Board

He who can take advice is sometimes superior to him who can give it.

–Karl von Knebel quotes

Advisory Board

Almost every business I had, had an advisory board. At first, it was unintentional, but over the years I've come to rely heavily upon an Advisory Board with every business venture. We got the idea to open a transitional living facility from one of our tenants. She was a recovering addict and talked about the need for housing for women in recovery. At the time, we had a 6-unit apartment complex. She told us what to look out for, what was needed, what wasn't needed and who to talk to for additional guidance. After visiting other facilities, we had a pretty good idea of what we wanted to offer and provide clients. We learned from the mistakes of others and used their experiences to side-step potential hurdles. Our tenant remained a trusted advisor in dealing with that particular type of clientele and we sold that business with the property, a few years later, when we moved upstate.

Not having any experience in the alcohol and drug recovery industry, we were called "newbies." However, with the help of our tenant (and another facility owner), we decreased our learning curve rather quickly and got up to speed on industry standards and what we could offer to set ourselves apart from others.

When we opened our contemporary art gallery, again, neither my husband nor I had any professional experience in the arts. But, we felt there was a need for more diverse art in the community and we were willing to stand in the gap. We had no art degrees; no art designations and neither of us were artists. However, we did know an art enthusiast and collector (our realtor), art professional (our realtor's husband) and had recently met a prominent local artist. I leveraged their knowledge. These people became our advisory board. I immersed myself in a handful of books on starting a gallery and we visited as many galleries as we could, in a short amount of time, and talked to owners, artists and curators. Almost everyone we spoke with was generous with their information and answering our questions.

This time, I made the board more formal, we went from 2 advisors to 5 and we met monthly for the first 6 months of business. I hosted dinner, acknowledged the board at events and included them in our marketing material and catalogs. We were fast learners, so meetings got scaled back to every quarter, and then we communicated as needed until the board was no longer necessary. We've been in business for almost five years. We've exhibited over 150 local, prominent and world-renowned artists, curated over 3.4 million dollars worth of work, hosted over 25 community discussions and received a community award. There is no doubt in my mind that without the assistance of an advisory board to help open the art gallery, there is no way we could have achieved as much as we did, as fast as we did and gotten the national attention we have as neophytes in an overcrowded art world.

I used the same process when we founded our solar cleaning business. Because this business involved new technology that was being used in another country and utility-grade solar farms were still ramping up here in the states, I leveraged relationships I cultivated from the gallery and enlisted a small group of advisors. The advisory board included a politician, an attorney, a lobbyist and energy professional. This time the group was informal and we met separately, but each of them was instrumental in bringing the project to the brink of fruition.

When you are starting a business that involves state of the art technology in a booming industry with new legislation and diversity issues, it pays to enlist political support or at the very least get political attention. However, be mindful of conflicts of interest when you are dealing with politicians. Because we were dealing with high finance, license agreements and technology, it was helpful to have an attorney provide additional guidance. The lobbyist came in handy for introductions and facilitating conversations across networks.

We ended up losing our investor and the market took a steep turn in another direction, but the relationships, wisdom and contacts that were generated in the process, were priceless.

Even with my current project, which means to support women entrepreneurs, I have gathered a group of professional women with a mindset for community and the advancement of women entrepreneurs. Advisory Boards, when implemented and utilized, can be what separates you from the pack and gets you to market in record speed. There is no better way to decrease your learning curve in business. You have access to a well of experience, acumen and insight that can be leveraged and used to your advantage; especially when you are new to an industry. Closing knowledge, skill and connection gaps with an advisory board can be all that is needed to fast track your business to market.

When I think about starting a business, one of the first things I ask is, "Who can I talk to that could help me sort through this?" You have to acknowledge your shortfalls, your gaps and your weaknesses. When you've identified them, you can then figure out how to offset them with a carefully selected Advisory Board.

Advisory board guidelines

Advisory Board members have no authority in your business. They provide non-binding solicited guidance. You can have each member of your board contribute their wisdom and experience to a certain area of your business or you can deal with the board as a whole for collective input. Either way, you need to determine what the purpose of your board is going to be. Is your board going to get you started and dissipate as you grow? Is your board going to be converted to a Board of Directors or remain in addition to? Are you going to change or rotate board members over a period of time? Will your board remain in place for the life of the business?

What is the purpose of your Advisory Board?

Your Advisory Board should be organized around executing your business mission and vision with a shared understanding of your objectives. Be clear about your needs and expectations. Understand your strengths, weaknesses and knowledge gaps and find advisors who can fill them. It's not required that they be experienced in your industry, but it is important that you select a board that will keep you out of your comfort zone. Each advisory board member should serve a different function and/or purpose. You want people who respect you, challenge your assumptions and will have a vested interested in your success.

Put the commitment in writing

Set meeting dates, time and location, expectations, compensation and guidelines from the start. Your communications and meetings need to be consistent. If your advisory board members are not geographically close, do video chats or conference calls. Try to keep your meetings to 90 minutes or less. Use an agenda. Stay on topic. Keep minutes or notes. Follow through on discussions and decisions.

Sometimes people mean well, but make commitments they simply can't keep. Having a written agreement that spells out obligations is generally enough incentive to keep people at the table, but you don't want to use it to badger people to participate. Don't be afraid to change advisory board members as needed. Sometimes people make commitments with good intentions, but fail to follow-through. If an advisory board member becomes distant or lacks active participation, give them an easy out and find a suitable replacement.

You want advisory board members that have your best interest at heart and not only want you to succeed, but want to be a part of your success. A simple agreement that spells out expectations and what your advisory board members will receive in exchange for their commitment and participation keeps all the cards on the table.

Compensate your advisors

Compensate your advisors (i.e. host a monthly dinner, cover gas/travel expenses, small stipend) with the means you have available. Most small business owners and entrepreneurs have limited budgets. However, you have to compensate those who are contributing to your development and growth. A meal and reimbursement for gas goes a long way with most advisory board members.

Leverage your advisors

Each of your advisors comes with their own network and resources. Carefully consider both of these when you enlist the support of advisory board members. You don't want to overuse or abuse their resources or referrals, but you do want to exercise strategic introductions and connections.

Put the **EXTRA** in your Advisory Board by featuring them on your website. If you are looking for funding, potential investors want to see where your support is coming from and that you have enlisted the wisdom of seasoned professionals.

Advisory Board Checklist

- ☐ Determine how many members you would like to have
- ☐ Develop the goals and objectives of advisory board
- ☐ Review your professional network for potential advisors
- ☐ Review your personal network for potential advisors
- ☐ Meet with potential members individually, first and present a convincing case for involvement
- ☐ Conceptualize structure, personalities and information flow
- ☐ Draft commitment agreement
- ☐ Write letter of introduction and request for participation
- ☐ Select monthly/quarterly meeting dates, times and location
- ☐ Draft agenda for the first meeting
- ☐ Draft an information packet about the business so that your Advisory Board can adequately discuss your business when appropriate.
- ☐ Generate mailings: letter of introduction, meeting schedule memo (dates and times), questions to consider for the first meeting, thank you letters.
- ☐ Generate minutes for each meeting and send to group members within one week of the meeting
- ☐ Send thank you letters
- ☐ Review actionable meeting items and execute
- ☐ Confirm Advisory Board members' commitment to follow-up action items

3 Start Up Basics

Ideas are easy. Implementation is hard.

–Guy Kawasaki, Alltop Co-Founder

Start Up Basics

Focusing on your purpose and priorities is what brings you closer to achieving objectives. It's so easy to be distracted and enticed by things that don't support your mission and vision. When you establish your purpose and conduct your business with a set of defined principles, not only is it easy to stay focused on your priorities, but you can quickly see distractions for what they are. In addition, you'll find you make better decisions when you keep your purpose, principles and mission at the forefront of your business.

Understanding why you are here and what you have to contribute to the world can be very eye opening, personally and professionally. It's like finding an internal home. A peace of mind that serves as a guide for making all sorts of decisions; large and small. Your purpose should be incorporated into your business. Who you are needs to be reflected in your business.

Every business needs an established set of values. Just like when you were a kid, your parents set your boundaries and beliefs (until you were old enough to acknowledge your own); your business needs a set of guiding principles. What do you want your business to stand for? What does your business believe in? These principles will set the tone for your business culture and consistently determine your priorities.

If you are ever unsure of what your priorities are, take a look at where you spend most of your time, particularly quality time. If you don't like where you are spending most of your time, re-evaluate your principles and values. When your purpose, principles and priorities are aligned, there is a certain flow and ease that comes with it. That's not to say that challenges won't exist, but the challenges are met with a clear and united mindset.

The alignment of purpose, principles and priorities takes practice. The more you are aware of the 3 P's, the better you become at maintaining alignment.

(See appendix for "How Ordinary Entrepreneurs Achieve EXTRAordinary Results)

Business plan

Business plans should be succinct, cover the essentials, referred to often, never be finished and always updated. Long gone are the days of 50-80 page documents padded with fluff and rhetoric. Business plans today are fluid, short and concise.

Your 1-3 page plan should consist of the following:

- Vision and purpose
- Problem and solution
- Marketing
- Operations and management
- Funding requirements
- Cash flow/forecast
- Exit plan

If you need funding, your business plan should include:

- Your team (who's at the table, why they are needed and who else you need to have, but don't)

- Product (what is it, how it works, why people will buy it)
- Traction (share your small victories - profit, revenue, pilot clients, non-paying users)
- Plan (what's your plan and why you need money)

Intellectual property

As they say in the boxing world, "Protect yourself at all times." If what you are proposing to do is inventive and/or original be sure to protect yourself with the appropriate copyright, trademark or patent. Be sure to employ NDA's (non-disclosure agreements) as needed and necessary. Very few of us have original ideas that require NDA's. Most investors won't sign them anyway. So before you ask someone to sign one, be sure what you are about to share is truly worthy of secrecy and protection.

You can file the required paperwork yourself, however, be sure to do your homework and read up on the process and what is necessary to secure the appropriate protection. If you are unsure how and if your idea can be protected, seek professional legal advice.

Put the **EXTRA** in your Start Up Basics with a mission and vision that supports your purpose, engages to your principles and adheres to your priorities and can be practiced daily.

Start Up Basics Checklist

- ☐ Research your industry and perform due diligence (See Concept Checklist)
- ☐ Set up Google Alerts for keywords, terms and name
- ☐ Select a mentor, advisor or Micro Business Therapist™
- ☐ Select an accountability partner
- ☐ Choose a name for your company
- ☐ Purchase domain names and secure social media names
- ☐ Set up social media channels
- ☐ Select business structure (Sole propriety, LLC, Corp, S-Corp, B-Corp)
- ☐ Write a one-page business plan
- ☐ Create a budget and cash flow projection
- ☐ Obtain required licenses, permits, patents, trademarks, copyrights, etc.
- ☐ Ensure you comply with government requirements (e.g., unemployment insurance, worker's compensation, OSHA, payroll tax requirements, self-employment taxes, etc.).
- ☐ Obtain Federal EIN#
- ☐ Open a bank account
- ☐ Obtain a sales tax permit
- ☐ Find business insurance
- ☐ Consult an accountant/CPA and/or bookkeeper
- ☐ Consult an attorney
- ☐ Set up your business accounting/bookkeeping (i.e. Quickbooks®, Freshbooks®, Intuit®, etc.)
- ☐ Select merchant account
- ☐ Determine supplier, vendor and service provider needs and set up accounts

- ☐ If you have staff, find payroll services
- ☐ If you have staff, review labor laws
- ☐ Create a website (Squarespace®, GoDaddy®, Wordpress®, etc.)
- ☐ Create and order marketing collateral (business cards, postcards, logos, etc.)
- ☐ Start revenue streams, acquire clients (See Client Service Checklist)
- ☐ Determine office space needs and requirements (virtual office options, coworking, home office, warehouse, storefront, etc.)
- ☐ Determine hours of operation
- ☐ Determine needs and purchase office equipment
- ☐ Secure your IT
- ☐ Create your work systems and operations (See Workflow Checklist)
- ☐ Determine smartphone needs and select appropriate apps
- ☐ Automate and document your business processes to create an SOP (Standard Operating Procedures)
- ☐ Create marketing plan
- ☐ Write and distribute a press release announcing your new business (See Marketing Checklist)
- ☐ Work your network and sphere of influence (See Social Media Checklist)
- ☐ Refine your product
- ☐ Refine your pitch
- ☐ Get to work and work your plan!

4 Legal

Lawyers are the only persons in whom ignorance of the law is not punished.

-Jeremy Bentham

Legal Entity

When I was preparing to meet with investors for my solar startup, I had to form a legal entity, get a Dunn & Bradstreet number, bonding, insurance and a bank account within weeks. I had to certify my business as woman-owned within days of that and I was competing for bids with major utility companies the following week. Forming a legal entity, even if you are a sole proprietor, is important. Give your business the respect it deserves by getting your paperwork in order. Know what permits, licenses and regulations are needed for you to be recognized as a business and business owner.

Research the various business structures (sole proprietor, LLC, Corp, S Corp, B Corp) and determine your preferred status. In some cases, you may want to wait to form your legal entity until after you have made some money. You should consult a legal and tax professional for details, options and consequences.

Work with what you have and improve as you grow. Start with the minimal requirements. As you grow, reinvest your money and keep things in order. When you need more detailed assistance, seek professional advice (i.e. attorney, accountant, insurance agent, etc.)

License and permits

SOHO (small office, home office) businesses still need to abide by local, state and federal business requirements. It is your responsibility to research and determine what licenses and permits are needed to operate your business. In addition to an Internet search, a trip to your local county clerk can help you determine local regulations and zone requirements.

Legal formation

Technology and the Internet make it far too easy to legalize your business. With sites like Legal Zoom® and Bizfilings®, you can formalize your business within days. These sites cover the basics. You can always amend and adjust your documents later. The more complicated your business, the more you need to seek professional advice. It's okay to use these websites to form your entity, but be sure to seek professional assistance to sort through complications and unique circumstances. You can also choose to prepare and file the requisite documents yourself. Only do this if you have done your homework and know what is required.

Banking

There is nothing more unprofessional than getting a client and not being able to take their payment because you haven't set up proper channels. Determine how and where you want to be paid early on. After you set up your business bank account, select a merchant to accommodate your clients' payment needs. Do you need to accept payments on the go, away from your office? If you are a retail business or provide a service away from your office, consider Square®, Intuit® or PayPal® services to invoice and accept monies.

Note - Keep your personal and professional funds separate at all times.

Professional advisors

Every business needs the services of professional advisors regardless of how big or small they are. Having a conversation or consultation with professional advisors from the outset could help you avoid costly mistakes down the road. Understand the business you are getting into and the legal, financial, safety, employment, etc. responsibilities that come along with it.

Put the **EXTRA** in your legal entity by completing your own paperwork and applications and have an attorney review them. Avoid hiring an attorney until you really need one. Download contracts, forms and templates (for clients, vendors, employees, partners, etc.) from the Internet and have an attorney review them to save on attorney fees.

Legal Entity Checklist

- ☐ When do I need to incorporate a company?
- ☐ What type of entity should I form?
- ☐ What state should I incorporate in?
- ☐ What is a certificate of incorporation?
- ☐ What are by-laws?
- ☐ What is the operating agreement?
- ☐ Is my business legally protected?
- ☐ Are my personal assets protected?
- ☐ Work with paralegals and affordable non-lawyer professionals and service providers when possible
- ☐ Prepare for independent contractor and employee issues, documentation and verification
- ☐ Educate yourself about legal issues in your industry
- ☐ Draft and review policies and procedures
- ☐ How will you protect trade secrets, client lists and confidential information?
- ☐ Draft website disclaimers

5 Money

You must gain control over your money
or the lack of it will forever control you.
–Dave Ramsey

Lean and Green

Don't let lack of money deter you from starting a business and avoid spending money you don't have. There are 1,000's of business that can be and have been started with less than $500 dollars. It's about starting where you are with what you have and making it work. Always cover your needs before your wants. Do you need the top of the line machine or can you start with an older model that gets the job done?

Draft and review a budget that meets your needs and covers projected income. Make sure your numbers are realistic and based on facts, not dreams and wishes. Use industry research to determine what people are willing to pay for your product or service and what revenue you can anticipate generating.

When you are just starting out, it can be difficult to make ends meet. Always try to reinvest in your business first. Recycle your money into activities and products that will strengthen and grow your business and help you do more, faster and/or better or reach more people.

Where's the money?

Help your clients understand your value proposition. It's not about what people will use, it's about what they are willing to pay for. It can be difficult to determine price points in a new business. Research industry standards, local competitors, online competitors, cost of materials and assembly time. If you are service based, consider value-based/ project/ package rates over hourly rates. It's better to set your rates modestly and raise them incrementally as you go as opposed to setting rates high and having to cut them to get the phone to ring.

Pricing

- Price for exclusivity – Offer your product or service to cater to a specific market or advertise it as limited availability
- Price for fixed costs and overhead - Determine what your costs are to run your business (i.e. supplies, materials, shipping, and include the value of intangible assets (i.e. convenience, time, etc.)
- Price for growth -Let clients know ahead of time that you are offering introductory rates and that they will be increased in the near future
- Price for free to premium – Offer free baseline services and charge for add-on services
- Price for the market – What your product or service generates in one market could be different from what it would generate in another

Metrics

Time is money and you need to know where and how your time and money is being spent at all times. That which is measured gets done. Measure your efforts so that you can make changes and adjustments quickly and easily.

Measure:

- Sales (and costs associated with the sale)
- Monthly profit and loss
- Client acquisition costs
- Cost of goods
- Overhead and variable costs
- Inventory costs
- Marketing ROI (Return on Investment)
- Social media connections and traffic (follows, retweets, mentions, shares, engagement)
- Website traffic (unique visitors, conversion rates, popular content/pages, etc.)
- Client referrals

Money isn't the only thing you need to measure. Other actions in your business can and will affect your revenue. Keep track of happy clients and use positive comments from clients as advertising. Favorable terms from suppliers can be used to encourage other favorable terms from other vendors.

Put the **EXTRA** in your money with cost-benefit analysis. Need to figure out how or where to re-invest in your business? Determine the pros and cons of what is needed. Make a list of the benefits that come with the investment and potential added income or clients and compare that to what it's currently costing you in sales and revenue to maintain the status quo. This works for simple and uncomplicated money decisions. However, for more complicated financial decisions, this will help you determine if you need to seek professional advice.

Money Checklist

- ☐ Determine capital and equipment needs
- ☐ Determine start-up expenses (i.e. marketing, advertising, legal, license/permits, training, staff, technology, insurance, shipping, benefits, etc.)
- ☐ Determine projected sales and revenue
- ☐ Determine merchant needs
- ☐ Meet with a professional advisor (CPA, financial planner, etc.)
- ☐ Create a budget
- ☐ Are there grants or small business loans available for your type business? How can you qualify?
- ☐ Establish a contingency/emergency fund, even if it's only in $25 increments, monthly
- ☐ Monitor your spending to determine where you can cut back and where you should invest more

6 Brand Identity

If people believe they share values with a company, they will stay loyal to the brand.

-Howard Schultz

Brand Identity

Your brand is a culmination of your business image, personality, experience and values. Just because you are a small business, doesn't mean you have to look or act like one. Your image, your brand and your presence speak to who you are as an individual and a professional. You are your brand. How you handle people personally can affect you professionally and vice versa. If you are a casual business, be casual. If you are a corporate business, be corporate. Be consistent. There is a fine and delicate line that allows you to be who you are regardless of where you are. That's where you and your business need to be.

Make sure your branding matches and reflects your actions. What is the perception of your brand in the eyes of your clients and prospects?

Professional image

Don't be afraid to reintroduce yourself to your public. Most people will connect you with a previous career, past job, etc. Your initial sales should easily come from friends, family and associates. But, closed mouths don't get fed. Speak your needs. Educate your sphere of influence on your new business venture.

There is no personal you and professional you, there's just you. When you are in business, again, what you do personally, affects you professionally and what you do professionally, affects you personally. Mind your reputation and mend broken relationships and bridges that will affect your brand in the business community.

People always do business with people they trust and people their friends trust.

Use social media to establish a positive presence and then cultivate it offline. Be mindful of your social media commentary.

What's in a name?

What is the benefit of people doing business with you? What does your business represent? What words are associated with your business? Why should clients buy from you and not your competitors?

Your brand needs to speak to your purpose and values. When people see your name, what do you want them to think upon? What do you want your name to mean? You are the only one who can give your name value. At the same time, you are the only one who can de-value your name. Regardless of why your parents gave you your name, it's up to you to make that name mean something within your business and outside of your business.

Your business name is an extension of you. I know there are some who disagree, but that is where the problem lies. Too many people want to separate their personal life from their professional life. Unless you want to live your life like Dr. Jekyll and Mr. Hyde, it behooves you to be who you are at all times. There is no need to "shift hats" or "put on your business face." Again, people do business with people they know and trust. How can people trust you if you present yourself one way professionally and another, personally?

Brand consistency

You have a great business name, it speaks to your product or service and you've paid for the domain name, obtained your business license and filed your LLC papers. Your market dictates that you use social media to connect with and sell to them. You go to social media to set up your accounts and the name is taken. How's that pit in the bottom of your stomach feeling?

When you consider the name of your business, be sure to check ALL social media channels. It's not enough to buy the domain name for your website. Your brand requires consistency across the board, especially on social media channels. Before I spend money on any domain names, I search high and low on Google and social media channels to see how and where it pops up. Although there are some rare occasions when you can tweak an existing name to your advantage, the general rule of thumb is to create your own and give it meaning.

Community goodwill

Community involvement (boards, commissions, sponsorships, etc.) generates community goodwill that you can trade on. A local presence adds value to your brand in ways you can and cannot see. People become familiar with your name, face, and brand and when your product or services are needed, you are top of mind. Take some time to think about how you and your business will actively engage in and support your community.

Put the **EXTRA** in your branding with consistency and professionalism. People care less about what you say and more about what you do.

Branding Checklist

- ☐ Manage your brand. Create Google Alerts for your brand
- ☐ How are you visually communicating with your market?
- ☐ Does your website match your business cards and marketing collateral?
- ☐ Is your typography and imagery consistent?
- ☐ State your experience and qualifications on your website
- ☐ Gather and share testimonials and recommendations from clients
- ☐ Utilize press releases and media kits
- ☐ Collect verifiable data and statistics
- ☐ Demonstrate capabilities

7 Tribal Marketing

Get so close to your customers "that
you tell them what they need well
before they realize it themselves"

–Steve Jobs

Tribal Marketing

Most new businesses have a zero budget for marketing. It's grassroots and guerilla-style. But instead of focusing on the ideal client, they go all out and try to appease every and anybody who will listen to them about their new business. The best way to connect with potential clients is to swim where they swim, eat where they eat, play where they play. If your client market is young moms, you can't spend your time mingling and marketing to men in technology. That's an extreme example, but give serious thought to who your client is and where they can be found. Where does your ideal client socialize, how do they find your product or service, when needed? Are they on Facebook, while you're on Twitter?

Find your tribe

Get to know YOU. Authenticity goes a long way. Know who *you* are, know who you want to work with and be where they are. This helps you naturally attract your tribe. It's easier, more relaxing and less stressful when you can be yourself. When you can talk about things you know and understand. Things that come naturally to you; subjects for which you don't have to constantly rehearse or explain.

I recommitted to being a vegetarian last year. I wanted to ensure my commitment was real and lasting, so I decided to write a vegetarian column for the San Francisco Examiner.com site. I already have a small business column, but thought if I publicly professed my vegetarianism, in writing, it would strengthen my resolve to stay the course.

I wrote a few sample articles, got approved for the column and went to work. I set up social media profiles, used keywords to connect with people in the industry and started communicating in the language of the people I wanted to be affiliated with. In short, I swam where my crowd swam, I spoke the way they spoke and I ate what they ate. I was immersed in vegetarianism. Within 4 months, I was receiving pitches from celebrated chefs and restaurants, I had been invited to an award-winning restaurant in San Francisco for a menu tasting, I had interviewed two current Bravo Top Chef participants, I received numerous product samples from various vendors, I attended a renowned food award event as press and I'm now working on publishing my first interactive vegetarian magazine.

It has been an incredible journey, due largely in part to my working theory (see appendix for "How to Market Your Best Asset") and social media management, which keeps me in and around my ideal audience and clients. The same system I used to establish myself as a simplicity and small business expert provided me with a respectful amount of traction and success in the vegetarian food industry in a very short amount of time.

Although the food industry is different from small business, this new journey also speaks to my purpose, principles and priorities. I don't have to over-think it and I don't have to work at it because it's already part of who I am. I share the some of the same ideals and principles that most vegetarians do. By incorporating my existing functional systems into a new industry, I'm able to jump to the head of the class and bypass the homework. The same systems I used for Simplicity Mastered™, I tweaked and used for Evolve the Gallery™ and tweaked again and used for Solar Hygienics™ and tweaked again and now use to grow The Vegetarian Aficionado™ column and brand. I'm connected to and have established some great relationships with some pretty phenomenal people in the food industry. I didn't have to expend a lot of time looking for them. Many of them came to me because my messages spoke to them in their language. I found my tribe and my tribe continues to find me.

Speak the right language

I read somewhere that a woman would always read or explain her product or service to her 80 year-old grandmother before debuting it. If her grandmother could understand and relay it back to her with clarity, she knew it was simplified and user-friendly.

You can't speak the language of your clients and peers if you are too busy posturing and talking about *yourself* instead of the benefits of your product/service or solutions it provides.

Your marketing language and message should include:

- What your product is?
- What is the benefit?
- Who it is for?
- and what is your competitive advantage?

Are there emotional benefits to your product/service? Do you have proof points you can include?

Keep your marketing strategy simple. Determine the outcome you want to achieve first. What is the purpose of your marketing? Is it exposure? Sales? Investors? Scale? Design your messaging around the desired results. Cover the marketing language elements above and include:

- A description and definition of your brand's personality
- Determine appropriate marketing channels (email marketing, social media, direct mail, cold calls, advertising, search engine marketing, Google Ads, Facebook Ads, sales team, trade industry events, samplings, local events, etc.),
- Create a marketing budget
- Establish the metrics to be used to determine the effectiveness of your efforts.

How do you know if your marketing messaging is effective?

- How are clients responding to your marketing message?
- Do they have a laundry list of questions?
- Are they confused?
- Are they asking for something else?
- Are they silent and non-responsive?
- What are your metrics telling you?

Tools of the trade

Get involved in the appropriate social media channels, professional networks and associations; industry magazines, blogs, podcasts or forums. Use these tools of the trade to disseminate your information to your market. Don't overlook the standards: press releases, public speaking, joint ventures, books, and referral/affiliate programs.

Cultivate relationships with the right journalists, bloggers and influencers. Don't hound them or bombard them with your information; but introduce yourself and keep them abreast of what's new and exciting about your business. Make sure what you share is newsworthy (i.e. new products/services and the benefits, events, industry awards/acknowledgements, etc.). Don't be afraid to ask journalists what stories they are currently working on. Perhaps you may be a fit or have a resource you could share with them. Most of the people who take the time to ask me what I'm working on for my columns, end up providing me with great resources and story ideas.

Know your industry

Nothing upsets me more than when a professional or business owner fails to hone their craft. That's not to say you have to know everything there is to know about your area of expertise, but you do need to hold yourself to a higher level of standard and know what is currently going on in your industry. You should be the best source for information on your industry, in your clients' eyes because you are *accessible to them*. You may be their only source for information.

Put the **EXTRA** in your marketing by getting out and talking to people. Power network to engage bigger clients and accounts. Social media makes it to easy to neglect meeting people face-to-face. However, face-to-face meetings are still the most effective way to engage clients. People want to know that you are real.

- Search your existing network and figure out who can help you get to the next level
- Request an introduction and explain the need for the connection
- Do your research; learn what you can about people before you meet them
- Look for common ground
- Prepare your talking points before the introduction
- Keep introductions relaxed
- It's best to meet in person or via video chat
- Find a way to return the favor

*If you are the one making the introduction, get permission first.

Marketing Checklist

- ☐ Have you analyzed your market?
- ☐ Define your ideal client
- ☐ Define your objective
- ☐ Define your keywords
- ☐ Determine your marketing strategy (i.e. blog, social media, video, webinar, podcast, etc.)
- ☐ Determine your competitive edge/advantage
- ☐ Determine your metrics and benchmarks to determine success rate
- ☐ Determine your budget
- ☐ Track marketing expenses and determine your ROI
- ☐ Determine your marketing message
- ☐ Refine your packaging and merchandising
- ☐ Do you maintain a database of clients, prospects and resources?
- ☐ Are you tracking leads?
- ☐ Do you publish a newsletter or email marketing campaign?
- ☐ Is your website up to date?
- ☐ Is your website user-friendly?
- ☐ Does your website have sufficient "calls to action?" (i.e. subscribe, follow, download, call, etc.)
- ☐ Are you on the right social media channels?
- ☐ Add past and current clients to your networks
- ☐ Are your social media channels and profiles up to date?
- ☐ Do you actively and effectively communicate with your local community?
- ☐ Do you actively and effectively communicate with your employees/partners?

- ☐ Do you actively and effectively communicate with media?
- ☐ Do you actively and effectively communicate with your suppliers?
- ☐ How often do you meet face-to-face with prospects, clients and business associates?
- ☐ Do you have an inventory of content?
- ☐ Does your content address the needs of your clients?
- ☐ Are you using auto-responder emails?
- ☐ Establish an editorial calendar and determine frequency
- ☐ Content is informative and up to date
- ☐ Review grammar and spelling or enlist a proof-reader
- ☐ Can readers easily find, understand, take action and share your content?
- ☐ Title and accompanying photographs or illustrations are relevant and helpful
- ☐ Optimize your content for search engines
- ☐ Include call to action
- ☐ Reply to comments
- ☐ Review and address your comments sections
- ☐ Consider interactive videos
- ☐ Consider polls and surveys for feedback and insight
- ☐ Give people option to subscribe to your blog via email
- ☐ Track traffic, monitor page views, links, comments and where content was shared.
- ☐ Refresh header banner and site images
- ☐ Monitor sidebar links for dead links
- ☐ Update pages

8 Social Media

Everything you post on social media impacts your personal brand how do you want to be known?

-Lisa Howard Horn

Social Media

Everyone and their momma should be on social media by now. Unfortunately, marketing is not about being on social media. It's about being on the *right* social media channels and cultivating relationships with the right people. Social media is a numbers game and I'm not talking about connections. I'm talking about the amount of relationships you can cultivate from connections.

There is no such thing as separation between church and state. Nor is there a separation between you and your social media accounts. We've all seen incidents of people posting things to their social media sites that come back to bite them in the butt, professionally. That is why I stress to my clients that there is no "professional life" and "personal life." There is just "life." When you try to separate your private life from your professional life, you are bound to expose one to the other in an embarrassing lapse of judgment.

Are you swimming in the Atlantic when you should be in the Pacific?

Being on the right social media channels is more important than knowing who your clients are. If you are selling contemporary fine art, you shouldn't be spending your time looking for clients and sharing information on LinkedIn. Art buyers are not using LinkedIn to purchase or peruse art. Retailers who rely on imagery to sell work tend to do well on sites like Instagram and Pinterest. Service providers tend to do well on Twitter and professionals and B2B providers tend to be on LinkedIn.

Again, know where your market is, how they like to communicate and when they like to communicate. Are they online during the week or on weekends? In the morning or evening? Are they more active Mondays and Tuesdays or Thursdays and Fridays? Get to know the social media habits of your market and set up your accounts accordingly.

(See appendix for "Why Your Clients Dictate What Social Media Platforms Work Best For You")

Social media management

Whether you are on Twitter or Instagram, most networks have a platform to manage and schedule posts. This saves you time and energy and allows you to focus on more important activities. Every Monday I schedule enough tweets to last me at least 3 weeks. Social media management for Twitter you can use: Hootsuite®, Tweetdeck® or Social Oomph®.

Social media management for Instagram you can use: Iconogram® or Followgram®. Note, if you are an image-based business, you can schedule, share and tag images that your tribe will be interested in or search for. Be sure to always tag things appropriately, but keep your tags to less than five.

You can manage blogs and news feeds with sites like Feedly®, Buffer® and Pocket®. Instead of clogging up my inbox with newsletters and blog subscriptions, I use Feedly® to manage information from all of the websites, blogs and news sites that I subscribe to. I go to Feedly®, read articles and schedule posts for multiple accounts on Hootsuite®. When I first started using Feedly®, I cleaned out my inbox in one full sweep. I was amazed at how much extra time I had recouped and how important emails were now more visible in my inbox. I was no longer distracted by unnecessary emails.

Take advantage of these time-savers and information management systems and use them with a deft hand. They can easily save you a minimum of 10 hours per week.

To blog or not to blog? That is the question

Many marketers and entrepreneurs will tell you, you need to blog to engage clients, add subscribers and stay top of mind. However, not everyone is capable of blogging effectively. Maintaining a blog requires consistency, sufficient writing skills, subject matter and time. It can be difficult to manage for new business owners. If you are not comfortable blogging to the standards required or you know you cannot maintain a blog so that it is useful, curate information instead.

Curating simply means you search for and share information that is useful to your followers and readers. Try aggregating and sharing information that is relevant to your market, clients and industry. The objective is to keep your voice and thoughts in social media streams. Sharing this information helps you establish yourself as a trusted resource. Curating relevant and timely information can be just as effective as blogging. Aggregating the right information can be just as valuable as writing your own articles. Again, learn how to utilize sites like Feedly®, Pocket® or Buffer® to collect articles to share.

I do both. I have two columns with the San Francisco Examiner.com and I write for Women On Business. I also curate over 6 active online magazines. Yes, six online magazines. The only way I am able to do any of this is with the help of technology to help organize and streamline my time and efforts. It's not for the faint at heart. It is work, to set-up. Hard work. But you can't argue with the results. Both methods have increased my exposure, followers, and readers and provided me with opportunities to push my message(s) to another level.

Put the **EXTRA** in your social media with Tweetadder. Ramp up your connections with a targeted audience from Tweetadder. Add, connect and reach out to niche, local and global followers. You can also automate and segment your responses.

- ☐ Claim your social media pages with your business name
- ☐ Know what sites are relevant to your ideal clients
- ☐ Establish your social media objectives
- ☐ Determine your social media metrics
- ☐ What are your client demographics (gender, age, income, location, income, industry, education etc.) and where are they socializing?
- ☐ Identify industry influencers, follow and connect
- ☐ Put the appropriate monitoring tools in place to follow conversations
- ☐ Create clear and realistic policies and processes for responding
- ☐ Create a content/editorial calendar schedule
- ☐ Create a list of keywords and search terms and incorporate into posts and articles
- ☐ Ask questions. What are your clients' challenges? What are your clients' interests? What are your clients' frequent questions or concerns?
- ☐ Connect to your clients and competitors
- ☐ What are your competitors saying and doing?
- ☐ Search relevant keywords and #hashtags
- ☐ Complete profile with appropriate image
- ☐ Set up business profile pages on Facebook, LinkedIn and Google+ (if applicable)
- ☐ Only set up necessary notifications (i.e. messages and comments). You don't need to be pinged every time someone likes your posts or shares your posts. You can see this information when you login.

Maintenance
- ☐ Update your social media profiles at least once per quarter
- ☐ Schedule tweets and posts via social media management platforms (i.e. Hootsuite®, Iconogram® etc.)
- ☐ Write at least 2 articles per month (proof-read) or share 5 articles from others per week
- ☐ Reply to messages
- ☐ Respond to comments
- ☐ Engage a couple of followers in conversation to cultivate relationships (weekly)
- ☐ Recommend someone to follow
- ☐ Refer contacts to each other
- ☐ Post blog post
- ☐ Post new products, services or events
- ☐ Post questions
- ☐ Respond to posts
- ☐ Retweet/Repost helpful, relevant or interesting posts
- ☐ Share a quote
- ☐ Connect with industry influencers
- ☐ Share an informative, educational or an inspiring video
- ☐ Share images (Instagram and Pinterest)
- ☐ Follow 10 new people each week
- ☐ Engage in 3 new conversations per week
- ☐ Comment 2 times per week on relevant posts
- ☐ Update Facebook (if applicable) 4 times per day
- ☐ Update Twitter (if applicable) 3 times per day
- ☐ Update LinkedIn (if applicable) 2 times per day
- ☐ Publish an article on LinkedIn (if applicable) once a month (2x, if you can)

- ☐ Update Instagram (if applicable) 3 times per day
- ☐ Update Pinterest (if applicable) 2 times per day
- ☐ Update Google+ (if applicable) 3 times per day

9 Technology

Productivity is never an accident. It is always the result of a commitment to excellence, intelligent planning, and focused effort.

-Paul J. Meyer

Technology

When you can streamline your business and operate efficiently, you are exercising time management. You are freeing up valuable time to work on core and revenue generating activities and meet clients' needs. Technology is your friend. The technology that exists today will be outdated by the end of the month. If you are not using as many technology tools as you can now, you are already behind. The trick and balance is that technology cannot and should not ever replace human interaction and contact. Use technology to offset menial tasks and time drains. But do not use technology to engage in conversations that require face-to-face or require a personal touch.

Website and landing pages

There is no excuse for any business not having a functional website. Even if it's just a static page, a website is a potential client's first search. We all do it. We meet someone or hear about something and we go to the Internet. Think of your business from the viewpoint of potential clients. What would you want to know, see, do or hear and put that into your website. If you want them to call, use your content to get them to pick up the phone. If you want them to purchase a product/service, use your content to drive them to click. Your website should be up-to-date, easy to read and grammatically correct.

Landing pages are a great way to engage potential clients for subscriptions and pre-orders. If you have a new product, consider using a landing page to test the market with pre-sales. If you have a new service or webinar, consider a landing page to generate registrations. Be timely with your information and be sure to follow up after the launch or close of the campaign.

Smartphone or landline?

Since the advent of smartphones, landlines are almost obsolete. If you use your smartphone for business in lieu of a landline, be mindful of your outgoing message and hours of operation and use of the English language in your text messages. Make sure your outgoing message is professional and includes pertinent information or sends the caller to your website for additional information. If your business relies heavily on phone calls, services like RingCentral®, Ruby® and Google Voice® can help you present your business in a professional manner and add a layer between your business and your smartphone with live answering, professionally recorded messaging, call screening, call forwarding and receive voicemails as texts.

Virtual Assistant

Business owners should be prepared to wear numerous hats to get their business off the ground and running. At some point, time and energy will get the best of you and prevent you from getting more done in a workday. You'll want and need to bring on help. How do you know when you need to enlist the services of an assistant? Revenue generating activities should always take precedence. If you are spending more time on menial activities (i.e. emails, social media, scheduling, invoicing, personal errands, etc.) and losing ground on the projects and tasks that bring in the money (i.e. client service, sales, etc.), you need help.

Just because you're new or small doesn't mean you can't afford an assistant. Sites like FancyHands® and TaskRabbit® make it very cost-effective to get help with small tasks that prevent you from staying focused on core business activities and client needs. Email marketing, social media management, ghost writing, scheduling, minor research and other time drains can be taken care of with ease by virtual assistants.

Billing/invoices

Make it easy for your clients to pay you! Use invoicing services like Freshbooks®, Square® and PayPal® to streamline and track your payments.

There's an app for just about everything you need as a business owner (if not, create it!) Use them wisely. Apps should be a help, not a hindrance or distraction. Always try the free/trial version first and then upgrade, if needed. Use them to save time, money and stay organized.

Put the **EXTRA** in your technology with apps that help entrepreneurs streamline operations and manage their time and productivity. See Wunderlist®, Trello®, Acuity Scheduling®, MobileDay®, Evernote® for help and efficiency.

Domain name

- ☐ Get as many domains as you need to protect yourself from copycats, but don't over do it. You may want to change your name later, if you're not married to it.
- ☐ If your chosen name is not available, look at other options like acronyms
- ☐ Ensure your chosen domain name does not infringe on someone else's rights/name
- ☐ Make sure your contact information is correct
- ☐ Set your domains to auto-renew
- ☐ Verify your information in the Whois database
- ☐ Arrange for your domain name to be "hosted"
- ☐ Create your web page and set up your email addresses

Website

- ☐ Site search is easy to access
- ☐ Major headings are clear and descriptive
- ☐ Company logo is prominently placed
- ☐ Tagline makes company's purpose clear
- ☐ Visitors should immediately tell what you sell
- ☐ Critical content is above the fold
- ☐ Site is easy to navigate and user-friendly
- ☐ Styles and colors are consistent and easy to read
- ☐ Use bold and italics sparingly
- ☐ Ads & pop-ups draw attention but are not distracting
- ☐ Main copy is concise and explanatory
- ☐ Include information about you, the company and team

☐ Can visitors quickly find products and product descriptions
☐ Make sure there are links to related products
☐ The link to place an order is clearly visible
☐ Full contact information can be easily found
☐ Number of buttons/links is reasonable
☐ Company logo is linked to home-page

Virtual Assistant

☐ What will you delegate?
☐ Where will you find your assistant?
☐ Are they experienced in your area of need?
☐ Orient your VA to your business practices and policies
☐ Provide clear instructions and guidance
☐ How will you communicate?
☐ How will you track progress and assignments

10 Client Service

Know what your customers want most and what your company does best. Focus on where those two meet.

-Kevin Stirtz

Client Service and Experience

Despite our increasingly casual nature in society, first impressions still matter. Always be prepared when you are servicing clients. Their perception is their reality. Every entry point to your business (website, phone call, business entrance, signage, social media, etc.) needs to speak to who you are and what you do in the best possible way. Customer service is not about under promising and over-delivering anymore. It's about creating an experience.

How are you communicating what to expect from your brand and service/product? Design your client experience around how you would want to be treated from the moment you interact with your business to the after-sale. Then make adjustments based on the clients' actual experience. Incorporate feedback from clients and address client concerns as they come up.

Always respond to client inquiries with facts, not jargon or double-talk. Listen twice as much as you talk. Be helpful, even if it's out of your area. Have a resource or referral handy. Don't give your clients the run around. If they reach out to you on social media and the issue can't be immediately resolved, give them a direct email address and respond quickly. Be as timely as possible in your responses. I know we all want responses at microwave speed, but reality doesn't always make that possible. If your business activities prevent you from being at the desk or near a phone, let callers know when to expect a return call in your outgoing message or auto-reply email.

Don't be combative or defensive when clients have complaints. Take it as constructive criticism and resolve the issue professionally and in a timely manner.

Testimonies, referrals and praise

Know how and when to share your success stories with clients. Testimonials, referrals, comments and photos of happy clients are valuable and go a long way. Leverage them on your website, in your marketing collateral, on your social media channels, on your blog, in your newsletter, etc.

Also, leverage your brand ambassadors and reward those who consistently sing your praises. If you have someone who regularly sends positive comments your way on social media or in your circle, acknowledge them accordingly with a heartfelt public "thank you," discount code, feature on your page, handwritten note, etc.

Be attentive, personal and appreciative

Stay top of mind. Keep clients up to date on your business activities. They want to hear from you, often. Cultivate your client relationships and exercise good listening skills; spend 80 percent of your time listening and only 20 percent talking, ask about business goals, ask what challenges they are facing. This is a great way to get a well-rounded idea on your clients' needs, interests and thoughts. The more you learn about your clients (and their needs), the better prepared you are to offer appropriate solutions and offer objective suggestions.

Put pen to paper

When was the last time you sent a handwritten card in the mail to say, "thank you?" When was the last time you *received* a handwritten card in the mail? That feeling that you get when you know someone took time from their day, to stop and not only think about you, but put pen to paper and send it to you in a tangible form can never be replaced with e-cards or a text message. Appreciate the value in personal touch. Find a way to incorporate a personal touch in everything you do. If you think getting clients is hard, think about the work that goes into keeping them. What keeps your clients from going to your competitors? Short client surveys and follow-up calls are excellent ways to gather information on your performance and your clients' experience.

Put the **EXTRA** in client service with a good CRM system (i.e. Batchbook®, Contactually®, Insightly®, Salesforce®, InfusionSoft®, etc.) and personal service. Everyone likes personal service. Treat your clients the way you would want to be treated.

Client Service Checklist

- ☐ Do you understand your clients' needs?
- ☐ Develop a client experience that focuses on value
- ☐ Create a client flowchart
- ☐ Establish written customer service policies
- ☐ What needs to be in writing (guarantees, warranties, terms, returns, complaints, etc.)?
- ☐ Determine how, when and through what channels to communicate with clients (phone, email or mail)
- ☐ Can you confidently explain your products and services, including components of products, features and benefits?
- ☐ Can you match specific products and services with particular customer needs?
- ☐ Learn how to ask for the order
- ☐ Who can authorize actions or changes?
- ☐ How long is your client cycle and can you reduce it? (How many "touches" before a sale?)
- ☐ How can you educate your clients on your products/services?
- ☐ Do you need to post FAQ's on your website or provide them in your paperwork? Are they current?
- ☐ How are customer complaints and conflicts resolved? Always be a fair and equitable
- ☐ Send handwritten thank you notes/cards
- ☐ Never discuss clients in front of other clients
- ☐ Who are your influencers or brand ambassadors?
- ☐ Do you have any client relationships you need to mend?

11 Workflow

The five essential entrepreneurial skills for success: Concentration, Discrimination, Organization, Innovation and Communication.

-Harold S. Geneen

Workflow

Know your M.O.

It's easy to get overwhelmed as a new business owner. Seasoned business owners get overwhelmed. Find your rhythm. Find a system and style that works for YOU. Take what works for others as they achieved success and then forget it. Because what works for them, may not work for you. But you could take one or two things that worked for them, something that works for you and put together something really productive and useful. If you are a night person, it doesn't make sense for you to struggle to get up early every morning. Schedule your mental projects later in the day and your lighter non-thinking projects in the morning. Find a way to work around the schedule that naturally works for you.

(See appendix for "Your Daily Prescription for Weekly Progress")

Putting your goals and objectives in writing is not enough. How you achieve those goals and objectives is more important. Put your tasks and activities in writing from the very start. Not only does it allow you to see what works and doesn't work, documenting your business processes prevents your business from falling apart in your absence. It also helps you prepare for future employees, partners and unexpected business interruptions as well as help you monitor and evaluate your business for efficiency and effectiveness.

Partnerships/collaboration

Being an entrepreneur and small business owner can be a lonely journey. Sometimes it makes sense to bring on a partner or collaborate with another business owner. If you have complementary businesses that can add exceptional value to your shared market or if you can reduce business expenses and overhead by sharing business space, it's worth considering. Two competitors coming together to form an incredible venture is not unheard of.

Strategic alliances can strengthen your business profile. Maintaining a short list of trusted and reliable resources you can refer to clients, can make you a virtual one-stop shop. You can also partner up for single events to provide clients with an exclusive opportunity.

Be mindful of who you let into your business. Not everyone is out for your best interest. People can be self-serving and take advantage of an opportunity to be exploitive. Partnerships and collaborations should benefit both parties. Efforts and leverage should be mutual.

Support

Do what you do best and hire out the rest. Hire people to cover non-revenue generating activities as your business allows. Interns, people who barter, part-timers and freelancers can cover the gaps when needed on a temporary or permanent basis. Be mindful of training time and needs.

Search out local undergraduate and graduate students who could use intern experience. Accountant, paralegal, marketing, PR, technology and administration are just some of the areas you could get professional assistance with the help of graduate level interns.

They say "happy wife, happy life." Well it's also true that happy employees make happy customers. Choose your employees, staff, vendors, supply chain etc. wisely. They are all extensions of your brand. Take a close look at the hiring practices and company principles of Trader Joe's and Whole Foods for examples of conscious hiring.

Accountability Partner

When you are an entrepreneur, nothing happens unless you make it happen. Business doesn't happen on its own. Your actions (or lack thereof) generate business or lose business. Yes, there will be days when you don't want to get out of bed or one click has you going down the rabbit hole on the Internet. It happens. You get distracted. You get tired. You get discouraged. You get off track.

Some small business owners know *what* it is they should be doing to sustain and grow their business; yet their lack of action causes their business to fail. Others may not know what they need to do to sustain their business, but are too ashamed or embarrassed to ask for help and their business fails.

You'll find that not everyone, including friends and family, understands your challenges as an entrepreneur. Most of the time, they just won't get it. This can add to your frustrations. A fresh pair of eyes and ears can help you see weaknesses and areas needing improvement.

An accountability partner can help you stay organized and focused on projects, tasks and activities that move the meter forward. Although they can't *make* you do anything. They can help you hold yourself accountable for the behavioral, intellectual and emotional choices you make regarding your business by calling you on your shit. Constructive criticism can be your secret weapon for making necessary changes in your business. They can also be a sounding board and a non-judgmental ear. An accountability partner must be genuinely interested in your success and have the time and energy to cultivate the relationship. They can be someone you know, an associate or a hired professional (Micro Business Therapist™). This mutual relationship requires candid conversations, respect and commitment.

Put your plans into action with the help of an accountability partner:

- Choose the right partner
- Set the rules, objectives and expectations
- Determine your metrics
- Set a standing time to meet
- Agree on consequences
- Look for learning opportunities

(See appendix for "Why This Person Is More Important Than Your Accountant")

Put the **EXTRA** in your workflow and join my Master ACCOUNTABILITY Group. A weekly call to plan, organize and discuss your progress on predetermined objectives. Each week you will have a clear agenda on your priorities, what needs to be done and where your time needs to be spent.

For more information, visit www.simplicitymastered.com and use code EXTRA2015 for a 15% discount or call directly (916) 287-1432

Workflow Checklist

- ☐ Home office or outside office? Is your workspace conducive to productivity?
- ☐ A desk and comfortable adjustable desk chair
- ☐ Adequate and appropriate office supplies (including dry erase boards, wall calendar, lighting)
- ☐ What are your technology needs? (i.e. computer, printer, phone, fax)
- ☐ Phone service (i.e. landline, smartphone, answering service, VA?)
- ☐ Create any necessary contracts, service agreements and invoices so you can easily bill customers, track payments and keep records
- ☐ Set up digital document storage (i.e. DropBox®, Box®, Carbonite®)
- ☐ Determine phone (RingCentral®, Google Voice®, etc.) Internet and software/app needs (See Technology Checklist) Quickbooks®, Freshbooks®, Wunderlist®, Any.Do®,
- ☐ Specialty tools of your trade
- ☐ Office hours and work schedule (what is your M.O.?)
- ☐ Document all of your processes and systems
- ☐ Avoid checking personal email or visiting social networking sites during work hours
- ☐ Schedule phone calls and emails during times that don't require your full attention
- ☐ Connect with clients daily
- ☐ Take breaks
- ☐ Engage creativity by changing your scenery
- ☐ Turn of unnecessary notifications and reminder
- ☐ Check emails and respond 2x during work hours

- ☐ Take mindful breaks
- ☐ Avoid social media surfing
- ☐ Plan your day
- ☐ Tend to revenue generating tasks
- ☐ Know when to say "no"
- ☐ Be mindful of deadlines
- ☐ Make minor decisions quickly
- ☐ Do your best work during your best hours
- ☐ Eliminate unnecessary meetings
- ☐ Determine your skill and time gaps and get support and assistance when needed
- ☐ Review and respond to your email at set times each day
- ☐ Only hold meetings that are necessary
- ☐ Create checklists for events and projects that occur often

12 EXTRAordinary Extras!

If you are going to achieve excellence
in big things, you develop the habit in
little matters. Excellence is not an
exception, it is a prevailing attitude.

-Colin Powell

EXTRAordinary Extras!

Friends and family may not understand what you deal with on a daily basis. Keep your energy and eye on the prize by surrounding yourself with fellow grinders. Join networking groups and organizations that challenge your capabilities.

Although your business is set up and you start to see traction in 60 days or less, Rome was not built in a day. Things take time. Overnight success often means years hustling in the trenches.

Get over your ego. Titles are useless. Be less concerned about your "CEO" title and more concerned about getting the necessary work done, meeting the expectations of your clients and building a brand.

Never rely on the "big fish" (i.e. that *ONE* big account or client). Diversify your risk, objectives and milestones.

There is no such thing as "being in control." You need to be flexible, nimble and adaptable.

Engage your local community for expedited brand recognition.

If you accept business calls early in the morning, late at night or on weekends, expect to continue to receive calls during those times. Don't be afraid to train people on when to call you or expect a call from you. If you make yourself too accessible, you miss an opportunity to set boundaries that allow for privacy and productivity.

Educate yourself on the fundamentals of sales, especially if you are an introvert.

If you sell an existing client a product, add a service. If you sell a service, add a product. Bundle your products or services for added value.

Refine your product/service. Refine your niche. Refine your marketing message. Refine your expertise.

No matter what your business is, the fundamentals are the same. Putting the EXTRA in ordinary is about simplicity. It's not about excess. It's about putting the right touch on everything you do so that it speaks to who you are as an individual. It's the EXTRA that makes your business stand out from the rest. It's the EXTRA that sets you apart from your competitors. Starting a business is easy. Running a business is challenging. Putting the EXTRA in your business is required, if you want to survive.

APPENDIX

Why You Can't Be Like Steve Jobs, Richard Branson or Mark Cuban

(This article first appeared in my San Francisco Small Business Examiner column)

You can learn from, train under and emulate whomever you hold as the benchmark for success. However, you can't duplicate their essence, their intrinsic motivation to hustle. That's why there is only one Steve Jobs, one Richard Branson, one Mark Cuban, one Michael Jordan, one Kobe, one Serena, etc. When they struggled and had to dig down deep to drive forward, that source is only privy to them. You don't have access to that. You can't borrow that. You can't steal that. You can't have that. You have to dig deep and get your own.

Your success is based on the course *you* chart, the effort *you* put in and the fire in *your* belly. You may be able to align yourself with the principles or ideals of another. You may even be able to use a blueprint from a path already taken. But what you can't do is get inside the mind of another and think their thoughts or walk in their shoes.

With people like Jobs, Branson, Cuban and the others, independent thinking, self-validation and a personal mission are what set them apart. You do yourself, and your business, a disservice when you try to think and do too much like those you admire. The quickest way to invite failure into your world is to compare your journey to another's. What happens when you mimic their actions and don't achieve the same results? What happens when you duplicate their process and it still doesn't work? For some, it's crushing. They will spend twice as much time wondering, "why" they didn't cause the same disruption. Why they didn't receive the same offers or achieve the same success.

What you could do with the success of Jobs, Cuban, Branson and the likes is use their experience as motivation, use their failures as lessons, use their wisdom as guidelines and use their success as inspiration. You invite envy and resentment into your life and business when you start comparing your path to others. When you begin to think, "Company A got a million dollars in funding, my product is the same or far better than theirs" or "Company B got acquired by Mega Company C, I'm going to model my business after them;" it's futile and faulty thinking.

Disruption cannot be duplicated. It can happen more than once, by not by the same genesis. You have something to offer. Something that is unique to you and your business. You have a purpose. That is what you should focus on. That is what you should cultivate and develop. Your success is determined by the path you take, not what lead someone else down a similar road.

Know your purpose. Set your principles. Determine your priorities and practice them daily. Your commitment and determination to your purpose will generate the "fire in the belly" you need to remain focused on what is true to you and your business.

How Ordinary Entrepreneurs Achieve EXTRAordinary Results

(This article first appeared in my San Francisco Small Business Examiner column)

We hear stories every day about average people achieving incredible results in a wide variety of arenas. Some of the most successful entrepreneurs who come from humble beginnings have varied stories, but common struggles and means of survival. Being extraordinary is not a birth-given right. It is something you have to activate within yourself… your mindset, your actions, and your belief. The only thing that keeps you from being EXTRAordinary, is you.

Ordinary business owners achieve extraordinary results by being attentive to their purpose.

We all have a purpose for being here. How you tune into and embrace that purpose could set the foundation for your success or have you aimlessly wandering from one career, project, location or relationship to another. When you fail to acknowledge, understand and leverage your unique contribution to the world, you invite distractions, heartache and poor habits to overwhelm your thoughts and efforts to live a life of meaning and purpose.

Sometimes we mistake our passion for our purpose. However, passion can wane and be redirected. Purpose is what drives you. It is innate and intrinsic. It supersedes passion. When things get hard, connecting to your purpose is what will sustain you and give you that "fire in your belly" that you need to push through. It will be that voice that reassures you and provides you with the direction you need.

Ordinary business owners achieve extraordinary results by developing a set of standards by which to exercise their purpose.

Being clear about your purpose drives your principles; your core beliefs and guiding precepts. Your principles are YOUR "golden rules." YOU live by them, personally and professionally. How do you incorporate your principles in relationship to your family, friends, associates, clients, your community, your supply chain, your staff, your colleagues and the environment? When you take this holistic view, your personal code of ethics and core values become fundamental. You operate and live by a single mindset. Not a personal mindset and a professional mindset, just one mindset that integrates your purpose and principles.

Contrary to popular belief, entrepreneurs don't have a private life. We have one body, one mind. They need to be united at all times. What you do professionally affects you, personally. And what you do personally affects you, professionally. Who you are and what you believe should be represented in all that you do, say, support and practice.

Ordinary business owners achieve extraordinary results when their purpose and principles determine their priorities.

With a purpose and set of guiding principles you can readily determine your priorities; the "what" of things you need to be doing to manifest your purpose and achieve your ultimate objectives and goals. Priorities are kept at the forefront and take precedence over things that take your eye off the prize; the myriad of daily distractions. The constructive benefit of aligning your priorities with your purpose and principles is that you readily make adjustments that keep you on the right track. Your ability to put first things, first, makes it simple and practical to say "no" to all that lies between you and your purpose and principles without guilt.

Ordinary business owners achieve extraordinary results with commitment and discipline

Something special happens when you align your purpose, priorities and principles with a collection of daily practices. With each passing day of living your purpose aligned with priorities and principles, you strengthen your confidence and resolve to contribute to something bigger than yourself. You become self-validated and empowered to live at a level that overrides insecurities, naysayers, fear and indecisiveness. There is a flow and rhythm to activities. There is clarity to your thoughts and ease to your efforts. Not to say your world is perfect, but there is less friction. Your capacity to endure is fortified.

An ordinary business owner with an extraordinary mindset can achieve remarkable results. Just because your business is small doesn't mean you have to think or operate like one. Ordinary people achieve greatness everyday. It's starts in the mind and is made evident in their actions. Today, think deeper and bigger and make it happen.

How to Market Your Best Asset

(This article first appeared in my San Francisco Small Business Examiner column)

One of the biggest challenges for small businesses and budding entrepreneurs is effective marketing on a shoestring or with no budget.

You can't get or do any better than word of mouth.

Word of mouth is mainly based on an impression you made with a client or a prospect that would like to do business with you in the future. That impression has value. You can trade on that value. And it all starts with contact. Start with your neighbors, friends, family, all the places you frequent locally, local organizations, associations, clubs, etc.

Marketing Brand You

You may not have any money, but you have something better—YOU. Use your passion, knowledge and personality to meet and share with as many people as you can—consistently. Start with small goals: meet and speak to two new or familiar people a day. Here are some suggestions to get you started:

- Strike up a conversation with people at your local coffee shop, grocery store, your kid's school, your neighbors' houses, or any other places you frequent.
- Call former co-workers, past clients, local vendors, or business associates.
- Email social media contacts.

- Visit your local chamber of commerce, a Meetup group, or local professional industry association.

It's easier than you think, once you try it a few times. Make a commitment and track your progress.

Start Conversations

Don't know how to start the conversation? Think F.O.R.D. (family, occupation, relationships, dreams). In any order, it's enough to get your foot in the door with just about anybody.

When you strike up a conversation with a stranger or a familiar face, chatting up F.O.R.D. is a great way to cover a lot of ground in a short amount of time. You can easily segue in and out of topics. You can ask questions that will provide you with insight on things that interest the listener. Use that interest to remember them, follow-up with them or find connections.

Using Business Cards and Handouts and Finding Complimentary Businesses

Don't forget your business cards, but if you are selling a product, have samples handy to increase the odds of them remembering you.

Samples are an easy way to get your product out there. Can you make smaller versions of your product for giveaways or samples to leave with complementary business owners who can share it with their clients?

Complimentary business owners are also a great way to start meeting and mingling with your ideal clients. Find local business owners whose services/products compliment yours and pay them a visit. Find out if there are opportunities and synergies that you can leverage to increase your exposure and attract your ideal clients.

Reach out in Your Community

Are there any small local events you can sponsor? Endearing yourself to your community can increase your profile ten-fold. Get involved with your favorite charity, volunteer your services. Help your community get used to seeing you. Become the familiar face. Your community benefits from your involvement and you benefit from the increased exposure. When your personal and business practices are aligned, you can organically attract clients who share your interests and passions.

Leverage the Power of YOU

Don't underestimate the power of YOU. Sure, it's great to have the finances for snazzy marketing campaigns and ads, not to mention being able to afford the professional services of a marketing or social media expert. But at the end of the day, it's your business and your product/service. Use your passion and hunger to get people excited about working with you.

Most deals are not made after fancy or labored presentations in an office. They are made over lunch and coffee. They are made after a casual conversation that leads to intrigue and excitement.

Think about who your ideal client is. Visualize them. Where do you find them? That's where you need to be. Get up, put on your best look, take a deep breath, and get out there!

Marketing on a shoestring or no budget? No problem. You have something more valuable—YOU. You're your best asset.

Why Your Clients Dictate Which Social Media Platforms Work Best For You

(This article first appeared in my Women On Business column)

Your client profile is not complete until you know which social media platforms your clients like to use to communicate and how often they use those platforms. Share too much or too often and you lose them. Share too little or every blue moon, and your voice gets lost.

There is a fine balanced line between informing or sharing and bombarding and overselling. You have to communicate often enough that you remain top of mind, and your message needs to be timely, informative and useful.

Do you know the social media tools of your trade? Where are your clients mingling, sharing and searching for information on products and services you provide? Do you need to respond with succinct messages, powerful images, or direct contact?

Facebook

Despite Facebook's market share, popularity and war chest, not everyone is using it. It can be great for galleries, not so great for cabinetmakers. Who looks for custom cabinetmakers on Facebook? It can be great for community centers, not so great for dentists.

Many small business owners are spending a lot of money on Facebook ads and fancy Facebook Pages and wondering why they are not seeing results. Nine times out of 10, the results are lacking because their clients don't use Facebook to interact or search for information on the product or service they provide.

Remember, marketing messages need to speak to your ideal client. If your client isn't on Facebook, how can they hear you?

Twitter

If you have a service-based business, you can pepper your tweets with tips, messaging, and information related to your industry, profession, and business. You can search Twitter for conversations on topics that interest your client base and join in.

With well-balanced Twitter activity, you can establish your expertise, develop a following, increase your brand exposure, and discover trends in your industry. Twitter is also a good source to encourage and support your colleagues. Many collaborations have been birthed on Twitter.

I founded a BlogTalkRadio show with three women whom I've never met in person, but met and grew to know via Twitter. We had a great time doing the show, and we helped a lot of people.

Instagram

If your business requires you to entice your clients with imagery (e.g., bakery, photographer, artists, restaurants, real estate, etc.), Instagram may prove to be more effective in communicating with clients and leads. The images must speak for themselves.

Hashtags help clients find your images and information. However, they should be used sparingly and must speak to the subject matter. One hashtag could be the subject of multiple and vastly different conversations. Search your hashtags first to help you clarify your references.

Pinterest

Creators, curators, and purveyors of fashion, stylists, salons, fine crafts, furniture, etc. will find Pinterest to be quite useful for inspiring trends and showcasing their personalities or cultures. Non-profits with a well defined cause and campaign might find Pinterest to be practical for sharing their compelling stories with images. In addition, magazines and schools may find Pinterest to be the perfect hub for their followers/readers.

Email Marketing

Don't let the adoption of social media fool you. Email marketing is still an essential marketing tool for every business type. You are speaking directly to your market, and your message should resonate with their concerns and interests.

Whether it is a monthly newsletter, a new podcast, a well-timed special, a new product/service, etc.; email marketing is your opportunity to get their undivided attention and have them focus on you. They have given you permission to contact them and share something of interest with them. Even with all the other chatter coming through their email, they are saying they want to hear from you. Don't squander it.

LinkedIn

LinkedIn is considered the social media site for executives, professionals, entrepreneurs, and small business owners. It is a place where connections are made, referrals are shared, and relationships are cultivated.

LinkedIn is for community building, in-depth conversations, and fleshed out topics. Business-to-business relationships are fostered. Job openings are filled. Alumni are supported. If your client base is reflected in any of these scenarios, you may want to spend a little time learning how to use LinkedIn more effectively.

Honorable mention, Angie's List

Although Angie's List is not necessarily a social media site, it is an effective source for many services and products related to the home (e.g., plumbing, electric, contractors, carpenters, pool service, etc.) You wouldn't search Twitter or Instagram for a reputable plumber. A well drafted and timely email marketing campaign combined with ad placement on Angie's List could be constructive.

For the Offline Client

There are clients in every industry that don't care for social media at all and prefer face-to-face and/or phone calls. Rare, but they exist. Please don't disregard them. They are just as important as your other clients, maybe even more so.

The extra time and attention you give them by meeting face-to-face or checking in via phone, goes a lot further than any social media campaign or activity. Why? Because it's personal. It's as personal as you can get. Not only have you taken time out of your schedule, but you are giving them undivided attention and they are doing the same.

Flip through your contacts and think about the handful of clients who don't use social media or prefer you call them, instead of emailing them. Rather than being frustrated because they require a little more time and attention, think about how you can enhance their client experience even more. I can assure you, those clients may be your best allies.

Your Daily Prescription for Weekly Progress

(This article first appeared in my San Francisco Small Business Examiner column)

The day of the week doesn't have to start on Monday. Just thinking about Monday, can bring on anxiety and anxiousness...and wanting to put your pajama's back on by noon. The word "Monday" signifies business hours, work, workday, and workweek. You can relieve some of that stress and anxiety with a little creative organization. Try working by a "prescribed" workweek. Divide categories of work among the days of the week for deliberate attention and real results.

Each day of the week gets its own agenda around a specific topic or revenue-generating objective. The undivided attention and channeled energy gives rise to productivity. Working in scheduled clusters can be just the change you need that is conducive to progress and direction. Here's my prescribed workweek. Sometimes the order of the day varies, but the effort and focus remains.

Day 1 | Reflect, plan and prepare

I use Mondays as a day to plan and prepare for the week ahead. Ever since I took Mondays "off" for reflection, planning and preparation; I found that not only do I get more done, but I'm more focused for the remainder of the week because I've clearly identified what needs to be accomplished within that time frame.

I set appointments, make a short, but important "to-do" list, research topics that will be in play, schedule social media content and watch a few movies. I don't even get out of bed until 10am most Mondays. It's almost like I know a productivity secret that the rest of the business world isn't privy to. Pick a day that works for you to start your week, it may or may not be Monday, and use it to reflect, plan and prepare for the remainder of the week.

Day 2 | Do the work including, administrative

Workdays are for just that… work. Not "busy" work, but work that is directly tied to an objective. Work that can be measured; work that generates revenue. On your scheduled work days, don't make haste of valuable time. Use every bit of it to push and move your agenda forward. If your objective for the week is to find new or service X-number of clients, then develop and implement an email marketing campaign, make direct phone calls, send clients "check-in" emails, ask for referrals, make "face-to-face" appointments. All of your activities should be centered on that objective. You spent the previous day in reflection and preparation. Now it's time to put the plans into action. Be sure to take an hour out of the day for tedious administrative work. Even an hour of focused attention on small but necessary administrative tasks will achieve great results… and keep you organized.

Day 3 | Do the work including administrative

I included 2 workdays because in order to start, sustain

and grow your business, you have to put in the work. The right work. Quality work. You may end up working 10-12 hours on workdays, but they are 10-12 quality hours. I guarantee you, when you are in "quality work" mode, time flies and you'll find you may have been at it from sunrise to sunset, but you made exceptional progress because it was concentrated quality work. I often work 14, sometimes 16 hours, a few days a week. I select playlists to match my mood on Pandora or Spotify and the music puts me in the zone. But those days are balanced by much shorter days connecting with clients, marketing, networking and rest. It works for me. It actually keeps me focused on what's important. I go hardcore on quality work activities for 2-3 days and then I ease up and refresh with the less intense days.

Day 4 | Client service

Many entrepreneurs and small business owners regret not having enough time to properly follow-up with clients. Taking time to check in on clients can be energizing and insightful. This is also a great time to handwrite a few notes of gratitude to clients who have been supportive or need encouragement. Your client service day should be about cultivating deeper connections with those very people who help keep your lights on. Stop taking them for granted and focus on giving them your undivided attention for a set period of time. Make it a goal to touch each and every one of your clients throughout the year at least once via phone, note, email or face-to-face. It's not that hard. Make a list, divide it by 52 and that's how many you need to touch each week. One day a week, focused on client service has a huge payoff. …exceptionally happy clients.

Day 5 | Marketing

"If you are not marketing or promoting your business, a terrible thing happens…nothing" said P.T. Barnum. I don't think he could have made that point any clearer. Marketing your business needs to be consistent and concise in the message and timing. You'll never know if your marketing activities are effective if you don't measure them. Know your metrics and understand how they affect your business growth and development. How many leads do you need to convert to clients? Which ads, tweets or keywords have been most productive? Do you know your client acquisition costs? How many clients do you need to meet financial benchmarks this quarter? Have you had more or less traffic to your website or blog in the past 60 days. Do you know why? What about conversions and lead to close ratios?

Marketing days should be a day of reviewing metrics, website updates, email marketing, designing and distributing marketing collateral (when's the last time you updated your business cards? Or sent out direct mailers?) social media management, and content creation and promoting.

Day 6 | Networking and socializing

It's one thing to be connected to 2,000 people, and something completely different to *know* those same 2,000 people. Networking is not about numbers, it's about connecting. Spend a day contacting and starting conversations with the very people you so feverishly wanted to add to your social network. You wanted more followers. Now that you have them, what are you going to do with them? You are going to get to know them. Don't know where to start? F.O.R.D. (family, occupation, recreation and dreams) is a great icebreaker. This also works well for when you are networking in person. The worst thing you could do after introducing yourself is to pitch someone. Forget about what *you* do. Get to know *whom* you are talking to. What are they like, what do they like, what do they need? Ask questions. Lots of them. The answers provide you with insight, synergies and opportunities for stronger connections.

NOTE: Day 6 is akin to Saturday/Sunday because networking and socializing should be casual and unforced. It's easy to find opportunities to network and socialize on the weekend when we are relaxed and just *being*.

Day 7 | Rest

Meditation, family time, spa time, brunch, dinner dates, take a drive, etc. Use the same amount of energy you had focused on work… on play. Be in the moment. Enjoy the company of friends, family, loved ones. Give them your undivided attention and bask in what feeds you emotionally. This is key to rejuvenating and re-energizing yourself for the start of your workweek. It's okay to leave the work …at work. It will be there when you get back.

Did you know your day of rest doesn't have to be Saturday or Sunday? Sometimes you can be more refreshed by relaxing in the middle of the week. While others are hustling and bustling around, stand still. It will actually help you tune out what's going on around you. Something we need to continuously train ourselves to do... pause.

TIP: Alternate the above days with financial days (review, plan and organize your business finances), new project days (devote specified time to getting a new project, product or service off the ground), etc.

What day of the week is the best day for *you* to start? Try operating on a "prescribed" workweek at least once or twice. You'll be surprised how much easier it is for you to focus and organize your tasks and activities. You'll be impressed with the progress.

Why This Person Is More Important Than Your Accountant

(This article first appeared in my San Francisco Small Business Examiner column)

There is one person more important than your accountant at the beginning and the end of the year. Your accountability partner. That person often looks like a business coach, business advisor, consultant or Micro Business Therapist™. Meeting with your accountant is imperative at the end of the year to wrap up financial deeds and tax concerns, and at the beginning of the year to address budget and revenue alignment. However, a professional advisor is even more important because they incite critical thinking, candid feedback and the necessary support for you to stay focused on what's most essential.

Reviewing metrics with a professional advisor helps to keep your expectations realistic, your practices honest and your objectives clear. Entrepreneurs increase their chances of success when they have someone who connects with them on a regular basis to review progress and listen. Here are some additional benefits of working with a professional advisor.

Accountability

The beginning and end of the year is a time of reflection, review and closure. Accounting metrics aren't the only metrics you need to keep an eye on. Someone needs to keep you accountable for your other business metrics. Take stock of your activities for the year. Compare them to your stated goals and objectives. Why haven't you achieved your benchmarks? What needs to be done differently? What needs to be expanded? How many clients did you serve? How many clients were lost? What new market could you tap? What new product or service could you implement? What is required to shift into the fast lane next year? What's the plan? A professional can help you develop a smart and relevant plan and hold you accountable for its execution.

Expertise and Experience

No one is too knowledgeable for an advisor. You don't know what you don't know and you never want to be the smartest person in the room. Leverage the wisdom and knowledge of a business coach, consultant, advisor or Micro Business Therapist™. Growing a business requires discipline, knowledge and commitment. What sounds good in theory may not be the case in practice. A valuable unbiased second opinion, sounding board and fresh pair of eyes can help you see what's around the bend, weigh pros and cons; and provide a perspective that serves the bigger picture.

Identify strengths and weaknesses

To step outside of your comfort zone, first understand what makes you comfortable. What's your security blanket and what do you shy away from? Perhaps it's people and large groups. Perhaps you have a best friend with whom you do everything. Perhaps it's a certain skill set that you frequently use or a job you've stayed at out of familiarity. A professional advisor can help you identify the things that may be holding you back and work out a plan for you to release them, while expanding that which gives you confidence and strength.

Connections and network

There is something to be said for "who you know." The value of your network lies in its depth and your capacity to extricate the resources you need and exercise reciprocity. Professional advisors can help open doors by introducing you to their network. Be respectful of their introductions by cultivating relationships and staying in touch. Don't abuse the privilege and remember, it's give, give, receive.

About the Author

Simplicity Expert. Professional Boot-strapper. Serial Entrepreneur. Micro Business Therapist™. The Vegetarian Aficionado™. Conscious Capitalist. Art Curator. Real Estate Investor... what's next?

My entrepreneurial journey has been nothing short of a beautiful ordinary life. True to form, I've experienced the highest highs and have been in the lowest valleys. I have had some incredible successes and some heartbreaking failures. ...I wouldn't change a thing.

Everything I learn, I openly give to you. I love sharing timely, relevant and stimulating information, hence my writing as the San Francisco Small Business and Vegetarian Examiner, being a contributor for the Women on Business website and curating online magazines including: Micro Business Therapy™ and The Vegetarian Aficionado™. I'm also one of Forbes 30 Women Entrepreneurs to Follow on Twitter.

The way I see it, entrepreneurship is your opportunity to have the work and life you want. Even when you're the boss, it's easy to compromise on the things that matter most. It's hard to know what direction to go or where to even get started. My goal is to help you make sure you're getting the most out of your business and that it is set up in a way that allows you live a satisfied, purposeful personal and professional lifestyle.

We have one mind and one body and I believe they need to be united at all times. What you do professionally affects you, personally. And what you do personally, affects you professionally. So, I practice what I preach. Being a conscious capitalist and a vegetarian helps me stay true to my purpose... living a clean, simple life and helping entrepreneurs (especially women) overcome the barriers to their greatest work.

What is Micro Business Therapy? Micro Business Therapy is the alignment of your purpose, principles and priorities with your business practices. It is a process that decreases the friction between your personal life and your professional life. What centers you, centers your business. What's good for you is good for your business. It is particularly effective for new business owners and entreprenpreneurs who feel conflicted, have lost their sense of purpose or struggle with "work/life" issues.

Join me for my Open Office Hours every Tuesday @ 11am-Noon (PST). Let's talk about it! Call me at (916) 287-1432 or connect with me on Google+ Hangouts

Need an accountability partner to help you stay focused and achieve progress? Join the NEW Master Accountability Group™! An accountability group for new and seasoned small business owners of similar and diverse backgrounds that meets twice a month for a professionally facilitated process that fuels improvement, growth and personal development. Each member communicates his/her goals, challenges and a set of specific objectives. Hard questions are asked and participants work together to problem-solve and be held accountable for their outcomes.

- Group meets 2x per month via private Google+ Hangout
- Individual sessions available
- LIMITED SPACE available for each group
- There is an East Coast group and West Coast group to accommodate the time zones
- Register at www.simplicitymastered.com

Don't let poor follow-through and lack of accountability hold you back!

Apps To Help Run Your Business

Client Management

Refresh
Sugar
Salesforce
Batchbook
Contactually
Insightly

Virtual Assistance

Fancy Hands
Task Rabbit
Robin

Project management

Trello
Quip
Podio
Basecamp

Calendar management and scheduling

Mynd
MobileDay
Acuity Scheduling
Tempo
Doodle
Setster

Tasks and to-do lists

Wunderlist
Any.Do
Asana

Personal Development

Coach.me
Couple
Mindbloom
Ted
Lumosity
HappyTapper

Documents

DocuSign
EchoSign
Genius Scan
Google Docs

Money

Mint
Expensify
Square
Freshbooks

Storage

Evernote
Carbonite
Dropbox
Box

News

Feedly
Paper
Circa
Reddit

Small Business Glossary of Terms

Accelerator: A business that provides rapid growth support to new businesses

Accountability: The allocation or acceptance of responsibility for actions.

Accounts payable: Money you owe to an individual or business for goods or services that have been received but not yet paid for.

Accounts receivable: Money owed to your business for goods or services that have been delivered but not yet paid for.

Accounts receivable financing: when a company uses money that it is owed as collateral for a loan it needs for business operations.

Accrual basis: expenses incurred and income earned for a given fiscal period, even though such expenses and income have not been actually paid or received in cash.

Added value: promoting an increase in the attractiveness to customers of a product or a service achieved by adding something to it.

Affiliate: A company that is controlled by another or is a member of a group, or either of two companies that owns a minority of the voting stock of the other.

After-sales service: Customer support following the purchase of a product or service

Agent: A person who is authorized to act for or represent another person in dealing with a third party.

All-in costs: the total cost of a transaction including fees, taxes, commissions and other expenses.

Amortization: the process of gradually paying off a liability over a period of time.

Analysis: a thorough examination of the parts of anything.

Angel Investor: An individual or group of individuals willing to invest in an unproven but well-researched e-business idea.

Annual report: The yearly report made by a company at the close of the fiscal year, stating the company's receipts and disbursements, assets and liabilities.

Appraisal: The value placed on the property evaluated.

Appreciation: The increase in the value of an asset in excess of its depreciable cost due to economic and other conditions, as distinguished from increases in value due to improvements or additions made to it.

Articles of Incorporation: A legal document filed with the state that sets forth the purposes and regulations for a corporation.

Assets: Anything of worth that is owned.

B2B: business to business, relating to an advertising or marketing program aimed at businesses doing business with other businesses

B2C: relating to an advertising or marketing program aimed at businesses doing business directly with consumers

Backlink: a means of finding out which web pages are linking to a specific website.

Bad debts: Money owed to you that cannot be collected.

Balance sheet: An itemized statement that lists the total assets and total liabilities of a given business to portray its net worth at a given moment in time.

Bar-coding: The process of attaching a machine-readable code to a product, package, container, or subassembly, and using a scanner to relate its location to the product characteristics.

Benchmarking: Rating your company's products, services and practices against those of the frontrunners in the industry.

Bill of sale: Formal legal document that conveys title to or interest in specific property from the seller to the buyer.

Board of directors: Those individuals selected to sit on an authoritative standing committee or governing body, taking responsibility for the management of an organization.

Bottom line: The bottom line is the profit after all expenses and taxes have been paid.

Brand: A design, mark, symbol or other device that distinguishes one line or type of goods from those of a competitor.

Brand ambassador: a person employed by a company, or not, who markets and promotes the products/services of a company within their sphere of influence.

Break-even: The point of business activity when total revenue equals total expenses. Above the break-even point, the business is making a profit. Below the break-even point, the business is incurring a loss.

Budget: An estimate of the income and expenditures for a future period of time, usually one year.

Business incubator: a business that helps new businesses grow and develop with professional services and space for three to five years.

Buyer's market: A situation in which supply exceeds demand, prices are relatively low

Capital gains (and losses): The financial gain made upon the disposal of an asset. The gain is the difference between the cost of its acquisition and net proceeds upon its sale.

Capitalization: the amount of money invested in a company or the worth of the bonds and stocks of a company.

Cash flow: The actual movement of cash within a business; the analysis of how much cash is needed and when that money is required by a busi-ness within a period of time.

Clicks and brick: a business strategy that involves combining the traditional retail outlets with online commerce.

Client cycle: The stages a client passes through including reach, acquisition, conversion, retention, and loyalty.

Collateral: property or goods used as security against a loan and forfeited to the lender if the borrower defaults.

Commission: A percentage of the principal or of the income that an agent receives as compensation for services.

Corporation: A voluntary organization of persons, either actual indi-viduals or legal entities, legally bound together to form a business enter-prise; an artificial legal entity created by government grant and treated by law as an individual entity.

Cost and benefit analysis: an evaluation and determination of all costs for a perceived value. To monetarily weigh the pros and cons of a decision.

Cost of goods sold: The direct cost to the business owner of those items, which will be sold to customers.

Current assets: Valuable resources or property owned by a company that will be turned into cash within one year or used up in the operations of the company within one year.

Current liabilities: Amounts owned that would ordinarily be paid by a company within one year.

Customer retention: The gaining of repeat purchases.

Cybermarketing: The use of Internet-based promotions of any kind. This may involve targeted email, bulletin boards, Web sites, or sites from which the customer can download files.

Debt/equity ratio: The ratio of what a company owes to the value of all of its outstanding shares.

Depreciation: A decrease in value through age, wear or deterioration.

Differentiated marketing: Selecting and developing a number of offer-ings to meet the needs of a number of specific market segments.

Direct cost: Items that are classed as direct cost include materials used, labor deployed, and marketing budget, and amounts spent will vary with output.

Direct mail: Marketing goods or services directly to the consumer through the mail.

Direct selling: Direct selling offers many advantages to the customer, including lower prices and shopping from home.

Distribution channel: The route a product follows as it moves from the original grower, producer or importer to the ultimate consumer.

Distributor: Middleman, wholesaler, agent or company distributing goods to dealers or companies.

Domain name: The officially registered address of a website.

"Down the rabbit hole": To be sidetracked by a change in events or distraction, to get confused or lost; off task.

E-commerce: The exchange of goods, information

products, or services via an electronic medium such as the Internet.

Entrepreneur: An innovator of business enterprise who recognizes opportunities to introduce a new product, a new process or an improved organization, and who raises the necessary money, assembles the factors for production and organizes an operation to exploit the opportunity.

Equity: Equity is calculated by subtracting the liabilities of the business from the assets of the business.

Exit strategy: A plan for how and when to leave your current situation/business.

Feasibility study: An investigation into a proposed plan or project to determine whether and how it can be successfully and profitably carried out.

FIFO: First In/First Out, a method of inventory control where the stock of a given product first placed in store is used before more recently produced or acquired goods or materials.

Fixed asset: A long-term asset of a business such as a machine or building that will not usually be traded.

Fixed cost: A business expense that is constant regardless of the amount of business being done.

Fixed expenses: Those costs, which don't vary from one period to the next; not affected by the volume of business.

Franchise: An agreement enabling a third party to sell or provide products or services owned by a manufacturer or supplier.

Freebie: A product or service that is given away, often as a business promotion.

Fulfillment: The process of responding to customer inquiries, orders, or sales promotion offers.

Gap analysis: A marketing technique used to identify

gaps in market or product coverage.

Gross profit: The difference between the selling price and the cost of an item. Gross profit is calculated by subtracting cost of goods sold from net sales.

Growth capital: Funding that allows a company to accelerate its growth.

Guerilla marketing: A marketing technique, the aim of which is to damage the market share of competitors.

Impression: A measure of the number of times an online advertisement is viewed.

Incentive program: An award or reward scheme designed to improve sales force or retail performance.

Income statement: A financial document that shows how much money (revenue) came in and how much money (expense) was paid out.

Indirect channel: The selling and distribution of products to customers through intermediaries such as wholesalers, distributors, agents, dealers, or retailers.

Indirect cost: A fixed or overhead cost that cannot be attributed directly to the production of a particular item and is incurred even when there is no output.

Initial public offering: The first instance of making particular shares available for sale to the public. IPO

Insolvency: The inability to pay debts when they become due.

Income statement: A financial document that shows how much money (revenue) came in and how much money (expense) was paid out.

Intellectual property: the ownership of rights to ideas, designs, and inventions, including copyrights, patents, and trademarks.

Keyword: A word used by a search engine to help locate and register a Web site.

Law of diminishing returns: Extra workers, extra

capital, extra machinery, or extra land may not necessarily raise output as much as expected.

Leverage: A method of corporate funding in which a higher proportion of funds is raised through borrowing than share issue.

Liability: A debt that has no claim on a debtor's assets or less claim than another debt.

Liability insurance: Risk protection for actions for which a business is liable.

Limited Liability: The restriction of an owner's loss in a business to the amount of capital he or she has invested in it.

Limited Liability Company: A company in which the number of people provide finance in return for shares.

Limited Partnership: A legal partnership where some owners are allowed to assume responsibility only up to the amount invested.

Liquid assets: Financial assets that can be quickly converted to cash.

Margin: The difference between the cost and the selling price of a product or service.

Margin of error: The allowance made for the possibility of miscalculation.

Market analysis: the study of a market to identify and quantify business opportunities.

Market demand: Total volume purchased in a specific geographic area by a specific customer group in a specified time period under a specified marketing program.

Market forecast: An anticipated demand that results from a planned marketing expenditure.

Market niche: A well-defined group of customers for what you have to offer

Market share: A company's percentage share of total

sales within a given market.

Marketing mix: The set of product, place, promotion, price and packaging variables,

Markup: The difference between the cost of a product or service and its selling price.

Mass marketing: Selecting and developing a single offering for an entire market.

Micro Business: An owner-operated business with few employees and less than $250,000 in annual sales.

M.O./Modus Operandi: Method of operation; a particular way of doing or performing a task or operation.

Multi-level sales: Also known as network marketing. Rather than hiring sales staff, multilevel sales companies sell their products through thousands of independent distributors.

Net capital: The amount by which assets exceed the value of assets not easily converted to cash.

Net margin: The percentage of revenues that is profit.

Net proceeds: The amount realized from a transaction minus the cost of making it.

Net profit: Gross profit minus costs.

Net worth: The total value of a business in financial terms. Net worth is calculated by subtracting total liabilities from total assets.

Nondisclosure agreement: A legally enforceable agreement preventing present or past employees from disclosing commercially sensitive information belonging to the employer to any other party.

Operating cash flow: The amount used to represent the money moving through a company as a result of its operations, as distinct from its purely financial transactions.

Operating costs: Expenditures arising out of current

business activities. The costs incurred to do business such as salaries, electricity, and rental. Also may be called "overhead."

Outsourcing: Term used in business to identify the process of sub-contracting work to outside vendors

Overhead: A general term for costs of materials and services not directly adding to or readily identifiable with the product or service being sold.

Patent: A type of copyright granted as a fixed-term monopoly to an inventor by the state to prevent others copying an invention, or improvement of a product or process.

Payable: Ready to be paid. One of the standard accounts kept by a book-keeper is "accounts payable." This is a list of those bills that are current and due to be paid.

Payment gateway: A company or organization that provides an interface between merchant's point-of-sale system, acquirer payment systems, and issuer payment systems.

Payment-in-kind: An alternative form of pay given to employees in place of monetary reward but considered to be of equivalent value.

Point of sale (POS): The place at which the customer purchases a product.

Price discrimination: The practice of selling of the same product to different buyers at different prices.

Product Life Cycle (PLC): The stages of development and decline through which a successful product typically moves.

Product mix: All of the products in a seller's total product line.

Profit and loss statement: A list of the total amount of sales (revenues) and total costs (expenses). The difference between revenues and expenses is your profit or loss.

Profit: Financial gain, returns over expenditures.

Profit margin: The difference between your selling price and all of your costs.

Pro-forma: A financial statement that shows how the actual operations of the business will turn out if certain assumptions are achieved.

Qualified lead: A sales prospect whose potential value has been carefully evaluated through research

Revenue: Total sales during a stated period.

Sales channel: A means of distributing products to the marketplace, either directly to the end costumer, or indirectly through intermediaries such as retailers or dealers.

Sales forecast: A prediction of future sales, based on past sales performance that takes into account the economic climate, current sales trends, company capacity for production, company policy, and market research.

Seasonal business: Trade that is affected by seasonal factors, for example, Summer weather or Christmas holidays

Seed money: A usually modest amount of money used to convert an idea into a viable business. Seed money is a form of venture capital.

Sole proprietorship: Business legal structure in which one individual owns the business.

Sphere of influence: Personal and professional contacts from a variety of resources (i.e. work, school, social activities, church, stores, family, friends, past employment, professional associations, etc.

Target market: The specific individuals distinguished by socio-economic, demographic and interest characteristics, which are the most likely potential customers for the goods and services of a business.

Target marketing: Selecting and developing a number of offerings to meet the needs of a number of specific market segments.

Telecommute: To work without leaving your home by using telephone lines to carry data between home and the employer's place of business.

Telemarketing: Marketing goods or services directly to the consumer via the telephone.

Trademark: An identifiable mark on a product that may be a symbol, words, or both, that connects the product to the trader or producer of that product.

"Top of Mind": Being the first in the customer's mind when they need your product or service.

Upsell: To sell customers a higher-priced version of a product they have bought previously

Variable cost: A cost of production that is directly proportional to the number of units produced

Venture capital: Money used to finance new companies or projects, especially those with high earning potential and high risk.

Viral marketing: The rapid spread of a message about a new product or service in a similar way to the spread of a virus

Virtual Assistant: A self-employed individual or independent contractor who provides administrative, marketing or technical support.

Vision statement: A statement giving a broad image of the future that an organization is aiming to achieve.

Wallet technology: A software package providing digital wallets or purses on the computers of merchants and customers to facilitate payment by digital cash

Wholesale price: A price charged to customers who

buy large quantities of an item for resale in smaller quantities to others

Wholesaling: Businesses and individuals engaged in the activity of selling products to retailers. Selling for resale.

Working capital: The cash needed to keep the business running from day to day.

Notes:

Notes:

www.ingramcontent.com/pod-product-compliance
Lightning Source LLC
Chambersburg PA
CBHW051537170526
45165CB00002B/770